BOOKS BY RICHARD KENNEY

Orrery   1985

The Evolution of the Flightless Bird   1984

for Bill & Kenny

ORRERY

*with thanks for
this kind hospitality*

*& with best wishes
to you both*

*RK
November, 1988*

RICHARD KENNEY

ORRERY

Richard Kenney (signature)

ATHENEUM

NEW YORK 1985

The author's thanks to editors of the following magazines, where poems, two under different titles, first appeared:

THE ATLANTIC MONTHLY: "In June," "Harvest"
CRAZYHORSE: "Easter"
HUDSON REVIEW: "Up Chimney"
THE NEW CRITERION: "Inertia"
THE NEW YORKER: "Speed of Light," "The Starry Night," "Slater," "Starling"
THE SEWANEE REVIEW: "Open Hearth," "Sweep"
VERSE: one section from "Hours"
THE YALE REVIEW: "Driving Sleeping People"

Published simultaneously in Canada by Collier Macmillan Canada, Inc.
ISBN 0–689–11631–4 (clothbound) 0–689–11640–3 (paperback)
Composition by Heritage Printers, Inc., Charlotte, North Carolina
Manufactured by Fairfield Graphics, Fairfield, Pennsylvania
Designed by Harry Ford
First Edition

Orreries

for Will and Tina,

who run the farm

and turn the press;

amores all

for Mary, though,

the one addressed.

Acknowledgement and Author's Note

The jacket and paperback cover photograph shows the first American "grand orrery," invented and built by the renowned Philadelphia clockmaker and polymath, David Rittenhouse. Like earlier European planetary machines, the Rittenhouse orrery was designed to model the movements of the entire known solar system, according to Newtonian and Copernican principles. The apparatus is unusually sophisticated for its kind, and somewhat baffling at first glance—Rittenhouse did not design his machine for "the ignorant in astronomy." His ivory planets are smaller than was customary in European devices, and set at a truer proportional distance from the sun; as in the sky, they're difficult to pick out. Saturn, at the tip of the longer arm, may be distinguished from the conspicuous gear-train driving it. The shorter arm belongs to Jupiter and its four largest moons. Circling closer to the central brass sun, each of the inner planets is carried along its own eccentric orbit by means of visible cams and ring-wheels. As designed by Rittenhouse, the main panel (shown) is sheet brass, 1.2 meters square, "curiously polished, silvered, and painted in proper places, and otherwise ornamented." Nine thousand hand-cut gear teeth engage to drive the whole system. Circumscribing heaven, the large silvered circle is really two concentric rings, the outer one fixed, the inner one moveable, marking zodiacal degrees. The silvered clock-face calibrates by the Julian calendar no fewer than ten thousand "Years of the World" and "Years of the Christian Era." It was intended to allow the apparatus to be "adjusted to any time, past or future," to the year, month, and day, "answering to that situation of the heavenly bodies then represented."

The Princeton orrery has a twin in Philadelphia, begun before the first was finished, and delivered in the same year. The two instruments were accorded high praise from all quarters, including such Colonial noteworthies as John Adams and the inventor's good friend, Thomas Jefferson. No encomiums to their accuracy ran more extravagantly than that printed in The Pennsylvania Gazette on March 28th, 1771, reporting that the clockmaker's creation "will not vary a Degree from the Truth in less than Six Thousand Years, if the present Order of Nature subsists!" When the world turned upside down shortly after, souvenir-minded Revolutionary soldiers billeted in Princeton pilfered some of the wheels ("handsome curiosities"); but despite these, and Einstein's later depredations against the sensible order of nature, the Rittenhouse orrery is in its third century now, and still runs.

Most of the information offered here, and much more, may be found in Henry C. King's compendious volume, *Geared to the Stars* (University of Toronto Press, 1978). Special thanks are owed Jay Colton and Gus Hedberg for the fine photograph, taken courtesy of the Department of Astrophysical Sciences at Princeton University, where the restored machine is on permanent display.

As for my own *Orrery*, first thanks to Max Hommersand for a lucky place to write it, and to David Huddle, whose lovely poem "The Nature of Yearning" shines obliquely through it. The centerpiece is a long poem called "Apples," engineered of many verses, some poems in their own right, each a miniature "orrery." If there's pleasure in the sequence, part of it ought to be watching them turn. Of course, it's one thing to see a small lunarium in the eclipse of a cooking apple behind its paring knife, or a modest tellurion in a half-turn off the wind and head's inclination to the lighting of a cigarette; for the fabrication of a grand orrery, however, heavier wheel-work would seem necessary. For this— starting with the magnificent, centennial, iron-geared, oak-beam cider press that drives their farm— thanks to Willis and Tina Wood, of Weathersfield, Vermont. Acknowledgement is due here not only for the loan of their machinery, but of their life and family as well, since the poem is framed through their eyes and set in their midst. Sifted from the hundred seasons I've known them (counting six a year in New England*), the sequence turns on that trick of memory which stacks our years like pancakes, perpendicular to time, so to speak, cutting through any number at once at a marked, recurring point. Nevertheless, there was a template year: one after Will assumed the farm; one before the press was repaired; the year Augustus Aldrich, at 86, disappeared into the fog on Mount Katahdin. As in any memory, the clockworks of a poem shaped to true events must play against uncertainty. For me, it was the happiest of times, spent as a guest of friends, working hard beside them at an old and unusual family business. Like small holdings everywhere, the Weathersfield

* Noel Perrin aptly calls the two supernumeraries "Locking" and "Unlocking"; traditional names are "Hunting" and either "Sugar" or "Mud," depending on one's temperament or occupation.

farm turns out just more than a self-sufficiency of many things; but since 1882 its main operation has been the production of cider jelly. This involves pressing apples, and concentrating the cider in a large arch-and-vat apparatus like the one used for boiling maple sap. What jells out of that is a dense, tart condiment once common throughout New England, whose manufacture eventually died out everywhere but on this farm. The cider mill itself is old, a relic of that preelectrical world run by complex mechanical gear-trains, tools linked by water wheels to streams, rains, and so the oceans and everything else. A comprehensible world, in many ways. The mill and its outbuildings are still chockablock with all these clanking, die cast, palmpolished bits and parts. Perhaps the fact that much of the stuff still works, and continues to do useful work year after year, shields it from the magnetic effect of flea markets, curio malls, and Museums of Americana. None of it seems to have left this farm, at any rate; and the clutter reminds me a little of the elements of literature— crippled dance steps, disassembled stories, half-hummed tunes, all common property— disintegration products, say, odd cogs and pawls, inert, cooling, fissile litter left over, with the confusion of much common sense, as it sometimes seems, from the decay of the clockwork universe. Or preexisting it, like the pie-eyed old acknowledgement we still mutter when we don't know whom to thank for luck or trouble— *stars!*—what I'll end this message with, since the expression seems to have circled back in tune with what little I understand of modern physics' flat circumlocutions of the globe and round heaven, formulations widening through every sphere, past poetry or politics, to lunatic strategic theory—

> listen— *tic, tic, tic*— there's watch-
> works for you. Consciousness. Uncommon
> wealth and properties, typeset
> in mind. . . . To punctuate the threat,
> a thankful note. *Tap, tap*— for these—
> a poem in a plasma bottle, say,
> cast so, then cast away:
> *Cap*: For apples constellating trees,
> bees circling the porch light, late,
> or birds or jets each other, *comma*,
> for the bullets wafting through this orrery,

ix

or lucky neutrons ticking through
the larger quantum china shop,
convention lets us press our eyelids
(green— red— blue— ah!
double space, in violet)
and thank our homemade stars, *stop*.

RLK
JULY 4TH

Contents

CONTENTS

CONTENTS

HOURS

Begin this story once again, behind the crown
glass window bay: another child unborn
and growing; apples overflowing bins
behind Augustus' cider mill— all ground
and pressed to pomace, soon, beneath the great
oak beam turned down, like night on day— on moon,
on sun. . . . And so the seasons in their grid
seem geared to this. The press has turned a century,
or nearly, here. And nearly dawn: the cincture
of the sun's ecliptic tightening toward noon,
and nightfall, dawn; while here, inside, the same sweet
light will strain the glass, pressed through the fret-
work of the sash, where life begins, at seed,
again: the blood-point at its infrared—

> To red at last
> cinder glows
> epicenter
> of the rose

So, genesis: a tiny yolk of russet
flame, spun flat, and cooled, cut square, reset,
to frame this farm— to frame this world— where all
light spreads at dawn this way: a blood-point whirled
around a high stone chimney flue, to fill
the eye and fill the mind and mountain-cobbled
well of sky with red light cooling into blue . . . the trope
again. And here's the burl of glass itself, a filter
on the world outside (whose every field's
a field of view), where birds rise through a cobalt
sky, and flowers puncture through the snow, and bald
earth on its empty screen— a spark that's felt
some breath of air in the black expanding bellows stir—
begins to flicker, flickers green light like a strobe—

3

Begin again, removed from Nature farther still.
Let's say this red-flecked changing field's the retinal
discharge itself, all rods and cones each day reset,
as sand runs back its upturned glass, and night, ink-
black, runs back its quill. We scry the distal
stars this way, through telescopes, that turn the tunnel
vision thus, from east to west, ignite
each dawn, and turn each daylight down to rest.
We try to take our measures so, by skylight squared
against its sill, metallic scratchings at the wrist . . .
time flows one way, it's said; and yet the queer
mechanics of our minds somehow arrest
its restless line— thus stars unburn, and reliquary
light returns, to grace the lacquered Almagest—

> Pollen sifts
> sand stone
> brandy snifter's
> palindrome

Time flows one way, it's said, and so a winter
night inert as quartz will come to rose-quartz
by and by. Who knows how changing fields
may turn behind the pupil's spinneret,
or come to green again? Not I. Inert,
in place, I've watched the screen; I've taken sights. I've reeled
in line from far-off stars, slack light wound backwards
into memory and night— a narrative
of sorts. If certain of these stars lie dead
along the dimpled curvatures of inner space
or time by now— the cindered net-work of the head—
inside this bay, they're lively still. Innate
or not, beginnings in a braided thread
are everywhere, and everywhere anticipate—

4

But *genesis*? The atom's eve? A simple clockwork
world, this farm, where evening stars and drifting quarks
spin lazily across the dark according
to the Laws— if Laws aren't blown to tesserae,
all microchips, a chance, a loss. . . . Say foresight's hindsight
backwards, then. A switch reversed. Who knows what traces
of the future, blazing dendrites, dance
in mind? If dead space accordions,
and apples shift from blue to red— they're Einstein's
apples, none of mine. I'll keep Sir Isaac Newton's
world, all crankcase cogs and whirring gears; Ikhnaton's
axletree's a god, here; sunlight's light, not curd-
and-whey. Who keeps the time in Janus space? Oh, blinkered
eye! What curvatures we're knotted in!

> Moonlight stirs
> marsh reeds
> noon and night
> the piper breathes

On limestone, once: a rare earth's sifting, oxides, ochers,
color blown through hollow reeds, how long ago?—
say fifteen thousand years, no less— Lascaux,
Trois Frères, Tuc d'Audoubert— to parse the time, to sieve
the gods, to limn the landscape in the skull. . . . Our cursive
lines all anchor here. And here's sand painting
once again: inspired, spun out across a curve
of sunlit sky outside the lung; here once upon
a time somewhere some lively window's piper spun
his spirit out in molten glass, each pane
a breath, a globe of flame, concentric with
the atmosphere— as every other sphere from birth
is bound to be, expanding on the current myth,
where every note goes flat, excepting Earth.

Shift blue: inside this bay, this winter annex
to the spring, the air is still. Stray tendrils
touch the handblown panes, where hanging plants
obscure the view. Outside, the autumn orchard stands;
its trees are bearing well this year. This time next
year— well, so they may again, unless, lanced
open on a rose thorn, say, the sun's red lens
should tear, should tear. . . . The summer's gone, I note. *X*,
Y: we try to place ourselves this way, our calends
and our ides. The sash rules out a net-
work square, its territories partly known, those regions
in the past explored. Identical
and each unique, each frame defines coordinates
without, within, the cross fire at its origin—

> Still compass
> rose boxed
> solstice come
> past equinox

Exactly *here*: sometimes I touch this turbid eddy
moiling in the hollow window's winestem
still, off-center, quick, a small storm's eye—
or still alive, like fish spawn undisturbed these hundred
years. Sometimes I watch the sun's red cinder
catch inside its glair, and change; or watch the moon gel
into form above the orchard's web, where hydras
wave, where hawk moths seethe against the glass like angel-
fish all night, some nights— until, like isinglass
against a kiln, the eastern lights refill, and scenes
of birds or clouds inspire their skies, glassy ciders,
lively, changing. . . . Touch the pane: here, trapped inside,
whole constellations of minute air bubbles seem
to rise, arrested in the instant of their rising—

Sometimes, as though they might pass through these trapped
and antique airs, attracted to the plants, perhaps,
the artificial seasons in this house, small birds
strike hard against the glass, glance to earth, lie stunned
a moment, quivering— the green untempered
panes themselves still quivering— and in that instant
held too long between wingbeats, the tympanum
undampened yet, its membrane rung and ringing
still (and still the bird may fly away)— I think
about the window glazier's whistling syrinx
and his airs, the false notes trapped inside this lens.
I think sometimes the shocked mind tries to navigate
such pockets, too, the pressure drops and turbulence
in memory. But this thought, too, anticipates.

> Lead screen
> red blue
> green lights
> riddle through

Transparencies: these windows hold their scenes like slides,
unfixed, impermanently stained. Sometimes I've tried
to pin them, pane by pane, a spindle of receipts
in memory . . . as though that wouldn't send the past
to shivereens! As though the cullet I've dispersed
through thirty years were gathered to the reed
pipe once more, breathed again, the thousand bull's-
eyes clear and newly softened by the hot passage
of the mind, the perfect ray of thought that flows
one way, and threads these bright syllables
of life like sequins all in line, as *such*
and *such* and *such*, until one image follows
on the one before, and time assumes the syntax
of a gunshot. . . grain by grain, discrete, intact.

So prescience cuts perpendicular to time,
I think, abscissa to the cross-grain curves of life,
as lived, spun off in rings around the sun. I've
counted all its annuli; the light I'm
lacing even now below the low
calvarium, its circuitry laid out just so,
in fine concentric coils: this is the smaller
orrery, the simple solar systematics
all our lives involve alike. As similar
as year to year, uninsulated lines of thought
may sometimes cross and come to touch— and then what static
light's released! Hot suns cascading ring to ring,
encaustic patterns, spark and spark, recalling autumn
in the fall, and spring anticipating spring—

> Begin recite
> by slow degrees
> how snows revert
> to verdigris

The seasons at their vertices. Appearances,
against a grid: black branches lead the handblown
glass, stained red with buds that bloom to fruit
that falls from pane to windowpane— transparencies
of sky to come, or overlays that who alone
may half recall, when the apple rolls against his foot,
an old man now, or now a child? The colors rinse
back out of view. Again grisaille. If life relaxes
into line, that's only gauging parallax,
X, Y, in time. All leaves spin down its labyrinth.
Why should we see above this maze, the blind cirque
of works and days, along a straight stitch of seconds
lacing back and forth our lives? Why should we scry
old almanacs, like this one, to remember by?

Now apple blossoms gone. Memorial Parade.
Now first strawberries burst upon my spoon, displayed
like fireworks scheduled for a month from Tuesday. Time—
Oh, memory is perpendicular to time, all right.
Near forty harvest moons lie stacked like plates
somewhere, with Christmases, and early snows, and late,
arranged by season, so— the suits in our Tarot,
where each card's punched and echoing. Say chimes,
which calling back and forth these verses now, relate
as little by proximity as cinquefoil, say, or a recent
rose, or one penultimate strawberry to the slight tang
of gunpowder adrift on Independence Day, tomorrow.
The berry calls to berries of another season,
doesn't it? As pyrotechnic *bang*, to *bang*?

> Doppelganger
> dropped to mind
> juggled apple
> lang syne

Since when? Who knows the physics of frisson?
Too hard. The heart's disorderly if fierce
beat plots awkwardly as lunar phases
on the sun's clear curve, keeps its own calculus,
all lock and freeze, free fall, light speed, all prescience
and memory *tic toc* on the same trick abacus
whose beads blink back and forth at will. There's no field theory
for these things. . . . The fourth today. The cider press
stands idle, here, its heavy iron orrery
at rest. Advance it, whirring: now sky above the orchard's
unripe apples verges up its own seasons'
scale, past violet, about to crack— circinations
in a handblown rose, held back at the point of flowering. . . .
A watchstem, *tic-tic-tic*. A second to the hour.

9

APPLES

an Orrery

Orrery

Just so: eccentric wheelings
of the maple keys,
the eelgrass levering
its quick, clear reflection
in the lake, the delicate
pawl-and-ratchetry
of crickets' legs— all gears,
a blizzard full of gears,
each fragile as a snowflake,
small enough to sneeze,
might so, in time, turn
this complex planet
from the sun
year after year
toward the freeze,
and never strake the heart
or the heart's green memory
a millimeter forward
from its ease.

Dream

In this dream
I juggle turquoise
apples. Dawn.
Between my brows
a telescope
is balancing,
suspended on
a fine hairline
of blue-green light
unbraided from
a rainbow's rope.
I've matched its swing,
in time, all night—
a thread-strung bamboo
wind chime
I'm the cyan
eye inside,
phototrope.

Grisaille

Binoculars
not dawn
ground fog fills field
of view— slow traverse— vernier—
now one itinerant
Jamaican apple picker
stirs across the retina,
resolving in the round
center of a Russet is it—
no, a Northern Spy.
Slim body still,
fingers quick as spinnerets,
he seems to draw the tree around him,
threading apples
in the eye.

Collection

Augustus is a pack rat: laundry
slips from the 1940's, filed
in boxes; boxes; scraps of tin foil
wrapped on candle stubs; old calendars;
back numbers of the *Geographic*,
Modern Agriculture, Grit.
String, of course; stripped bolts; odd bits
of wire; a clutch of defunct traffic
tickets spindled on a pitchfork tine;
old clocks and sprung watches squirrelled
away against some future time,
some swept, spare, less provident world—

Garden

Eclectic archaeology, indeed,
collector's paradise; and yet the true
life's work lies outside, in the reliquary
orchard old Augustus Aldrich grew:
some fifty rare varieties, a hundred
stems all told— his ark of apples, two
by two. The long curatorship is done
now; trees are running wild. I watch the sun
rise up behind the ranks and files, project
its cone of light down on this queer Mercator
map of one man's dead desire; I mark
the equinoxes by a single tree.
I try my best to bring them back— recite,
now: *Stamen, Winesap, Northern Spy, Rome
Russet, Blue Permaine*— I've heard Augustus
speak them through; I can't recall the names.

Inertia

Equinox again. I sit
at rest, with whiskey, on the porch—
and nightfall, equal, opposite—
and ponder ostriches who, planted
earthwise, feathered as this orchard
is, have donned the planetary
helmet, like a fishbowl, upside
down. So dizzying. I wish
I understood the calendar
that turns me too, as blind, as blind—
what rest we keep relinquishing!
Now apple trees are paper lanterns
candled by the sun behind
them. Winter, soon. They tear. Wind-torn,
a few of them reveal the wick
itself, before it dies. A few spent
bees lift off the porch light, turn
a dazed ecliptic down. They walk
a little on the cold cement;
by morning they'll have died, no doubt.
By spring the lantern's light blown out
may light anew, and trees will mend,
as orchard comes to bloom again—
I skirt the bees on my way inside.
I circle too, you see; I'll ride
the slight curve generated here
out to the very end— to bed,
where breath will fail to close the sphere
of dark-to-light around my head—
Hush, hush, you'll say, *the harsher laws*
of motion, love, can never govern
our emotion. Loss by loss,
love conserves— its fine vernier
is at your touch. I feel its solace
settle here; your arms by turns
encircle me, to stillness, nearly,
for a moment, nightfall turbanned
round and round . . . a vernal solstice
at the soul. And then again the veer—

The Golden Bough

Millard checks his pocket piece. *Just passed,*
he says. On with the biannual pyromantic forecast.
Scratch; scratch. Irwin's wife's mother's witchcraft
warns *when the sun is due to cross the Line, watch*
which way the smoke inclines. No robes; no sacrifice;
no sacred mistletoe; two neighbors fossicking
for news without much talk— no mystery since March—
mark their equinox this way: high on a tractor
seat (just back from the doctor, *damned thief,* faith in burdock
tea rekindled), *contact:* Irwin's last damp kitchen match
consecrates an empty Agway feed sack.
Zeus, reduced. He whirls it around his head 'til it flowers
flame, flings it with a furrowed brow to the sodden
roadside. We watch it hiss and smolder, the smoke's sour
snake upweaving to no particular charmer . . . moot
smoke. Maybe ribbons off uncertainly
southeastward, now. Irwin's wife mutters *sure to*
be a cold winter. Irwin shakes his head, *shoot*
there's not a man on earth worth ten dollars an hour.

Open Hearth

Old chimney leading nowhere, leaking
light between two walls. Oblique
and sooty light, unseen— what limns
a long-lost manuscript, the vellum
of the living bat wing, veined
and warm, and waving like a seine
of tattered cob-silk in the sift
of draft walled in since eighteen fifty-
nine (Augustan reckoning;
we don't discuss it). *Use the wrecking
bar. Break in. We'll tap that flue
again*, he says; and so we do.
We tear through plaster, lath, expose
the frame, the joiner's simple post-
and-beam, where geometric scratch-marks
match (odd symbols, one man's arcane
catalogue, attracting tenons
to their mortises); in ten
short minutes here we flay the old house
back to masonry, and douse
the dark again, and lay the square
of sunlight on the old hearth bare.
Ah, *mystery*! I've half imagined
ancient palm prints pressed here, matching
mine— across the antique fireback's
upcurve, ochres, umbers, black-
on-black— a man's breath blowing colored
pigments through the reed-pipe, curling
smoke, a russet bloom— oh, flesh
in waves by torchlight, half lit, flanks fletched
with arrows willed there by a bird-masked
man, an antlered man . . . wild musk-
ox, aurochs, reindeer, snowy owl—
and eyes below dead eyes, skin cowls
pulled close around their brows, old ice-
men, stalking down the stone horizons
of the Pleistocene when earth
was opened, unswept as this hearth—
old ash-bed sprinkled by the rain,
where eyes first opened into flame—

Augustus Boiling

Feed the fire. A small apocalypse
outside, the sun goes down behind the orchard—
jellied gasoline— slips through the branches
slowly, leaving droplets, blebs, bright apples
of itself behind. I swing iron hinges,
toss a cracked jar into the roaring arch,
watch it dimple and relax, an orange
gobbet full of flame. Doors clang shut.
The cider chuckles, thickening. Steam sheets
up off the copper pan, and I can scarcely
see Augustus there, five rheumy feet across
from me. Sweet cider fills our mackinaws,
our skins, our beards, our dreams at night, the air.
We drain the boiled concentrate in jars.
It jells. We do not speak. The autumn stars
tic-toc— the telltale heart, I think. We stare.

After Late Work, Before Sleep

Orion's back, Augustus said. Look up.
Calm, cool now, late; fires all but dead.
Augustus silent down the path;
no other speech passed;
I don't try to catch him. Stop.
Struck match makes a perfect globe, cupped
so in my palms . . .
deliquescent moon rides low in a pool of clouds,
and I blow smoke rings at its horns.
Below the moon,
the yellow oblong of our room—
its light strains out through torn screens
(storms soon; take note).
Stairs seem steep.
Trouser buckle bells loud on bare floor boards.
Cool crescent of your back
is smooth against my chest and belly
sleep

Dream

I seem to juggle green apples
in the crown pane;
a dream of new breath tippled up
on stems of green champagne,
where bubbles rise the glassy flue
like notes blown off a reed,
or once and future zeroes through
the ephemerides.

Escape

This evening we've escaped the close house,
Augustus' laundry hanging in the kitchen—
all of that— to dance. Here circles form,
unform, to squares; here fiddles, concertina,
dulcimer, assorted spoons and tin
whistles, a set of uilleann pipes. The piper
sits erect, absorbed. His elbow crooks
and flaps; the bellows fill, the bladder swells
and dimples, swells, it buzzes like a flytrap
closed, a pitcher plant digesting bees . . .
his fingers on the chanter lift, and notes
whine up into the rafters, streaming tails
against the breeze—
                    We set and swing. The Scottish
ballads and the contra dance recall
the minutes of our first acquaintance, caught
in the turning plexus of an unfamiliar
reel— how awkwardness attracts!— how trapped
inside the wheeling set we ricochetted
like daystruck bats, until we'd learned the time
by turns, the whorls inside its orrery,
the ticking of the *pas de basque*—
                                    Now listen
to the chanter, turn with me, and close
your eyes: the figures of the dance unlace
like snowflakes, caught in a cupped palm, gone. The drones
trail off—
          And driving home beneath a starry
night grown turbulent itself, the warm sky
bellying like cheesecloth through the open
windows, half-moon uncollapsing over
us, a gravid pipe-skin, too— and holding
hands, returning home, we lurch into
the breezy line-dance of the laundry, arm
in arm, the empty dead. I think about
the breathing pipes tonight, my love, the slow
heart reeding its catarrhal changes, flowers
changing in a sheep's stomach, cider changing
in its cask two floors below your bed—

Geometry

And blood, too,
what wreathing through
our families
escapes one way
like every other
changing thing
in earth, but thought,
into the future
from the past.
And where these cross—
an intercept,
the dancer's knot,
the piper's breath
shaped into snowflakes
in the syrinx
caught between
two skins of dark
and turbid air—
or say sand
sifting back
its vortex, trapped,
coincident
in us, an instant;
passing then,
then passed— and what
must be the child
but this, a small
geometry
of dust and charge,
a small disturbance,
dense and quick,
a pluming at
the iris of
a steeply curving glass—

Augustus Grinding

Sweet dark upstairs in the barn,
both zebra-striped, Venetian blind
in the bright strobe-sunlight shafting through
the slatted boards, we work this mine.
Sudden hands and faces gleam
like apples halved on a shovel's edge.
Thud thud thud— so, by the hundreds
apples drum down the wooden
chute— short work, rewarded
with the rabid, strangled, foam-
flecked snoring in the grinder. I try
to fill the dimple in this sea
of apples sucking quickly through
to sweet spray down their drain and growing
cone of macerated pulp
below; a rapid transformation—
one I'd just as soon postpone,
and so take care, keep well away
from the flashing vortex, facing towards
it, feeding, feeding; while Augustus
stalks these dwindling bins, bent double
like some grim larcenous dwarf,
hotly loading up his scuttles
full of rubies, while the dragon
snarls asleep on the lower slopes
of his broken pomegranate hoard.

Harvest

Bounty, bounty!
Silver corn husks cracked down by fat raccoons,
pumpkins squat amidst the sift and fall of seeds,
racks of acorn squash collapsed,
tomatoes split and leaking in the boggy tangle of their vines,
apples bruising in their bins,
the half Harvest Moon itself
a tipped snifter—
I incline my chin.

Augustus Pressing

This mill was by the river, once;
I've seen Augustus' photographs:
stately water wheel revolving,
cider press and querns inside
all running off a single shaft
by leather belts. The Army Corps
of Engineers has built a dam;
we've lost ground; all gone.
It's four hands on a long pole, now— up,
down. The cast iron ratchet clicks
its axle, pivot gears and worm-
screws earn their quarter inch; a sheet
of cider curtains gleaming off
the sluiceboard, *ssssshh.* Up, down, and *ssssshh,*
all morning long, with maple keys,
and cumuli like heavy querns
on the cut fields, geese like smoke
in the flyways, *ssssshh,* and grey November
coming down by quarter-turns.

Lord Protector

Something's taking hens this fall—
feathers in the coop, broken eggs.
Last night I went out with a flashlight,
caught them, seething on the floor:
rats. They ambled off indifferently.
Not far above, by the only king
post in the building, sat the rooster,
hardly himself. He'd seen what he'd seen.
He spends his afternoons now drunk
on pomace piled outside the cider
mill where it ferments. He crows,
lurches like a stage drunk, crows
again, warming his feet in the yeasty
pomace, numbering his days.

Crosshairs

Day one
full Hunter's Moon bears
slowly down to treeline
crosshairs
in a lead glass lens
streak sunrise
like the muzzle's bloom
to red wine red meat
run
this hunting season's
on us now and noon
and well begun
deer hung
from maple trees see
how they've come to town
they line the streets
each shrinks around
its singularity
a seed discrete
sewn thoughtfully in earth
undone
and still the clear dome
ringing like a goblet
with the sound
sun
a spent shell casing
smoking on the newly
frozen ground
gone
now darkness once again
fine crosshairs
here a spikehorn buck
strung upside down
still warm
between his points
a spider spins by starlight
dewdrops form
dark ebbs
to dawn I feel the breeze

the planets pulsing
in their web
the moon
an edged flake sharp Orion's
broadhead
hear the torn
sky wind the heartbeat blood
what congruence
of fear
what spiralling
to morning is the inner
ear in him
the rifled cochlea
the Hunter's
clear and dreadful horn

Shadow

Earlier today, we watched hawks
orbiting the rock-walled upper pasture,
　　quartering its open ground,
and I imagined how the harsh transfer
　　might happen: star-nosed mole refigured
perfectly, its pink creased eyes, hydra
　　snout, its splay feet clay-crumbed, fur
patchy; the whole mole blazing, isolate,
　　completed on the back curve
of the black volcanic bead in the bird's orbit—

Outside the window now, our son is playing
　　in the orchard. I tell my wife
I think a daughter this time; this time (so
　　I think) my wife will disagree—
who quick and awkward starts up, interrupts
　　me, twisting on her chair— to what?
A commonplace: a child's inexpert leap
　　for a low apple; loose sleeve
caught, and tree's talons following down fast. . . .
　　The branch plucks free, of course, springs back—

　　this is New England, after all.
There's never been *accipiter* enough
　　in these close skies for quite so much
adrenaline; and still we feel it, feel
　　against our faces wind, wings'
last-second braking, furl, the sharp shock
　　in the chest, and then— a long, slow
spiralling, maybe. . . . He'll dream this, too,
　　maybe. Who monitors his nightmares
now? I know I keep the shadow in me,

angular and black, unclearly known;
　　if known, unnamed. Some long-dead raptor's
gyre and stoop. I search for the source of this,
　　stone blind and sweeping bare palms
on the marble floor of sleep for this,
　　for some sharp gnomon's broken point,

some dense sliver of volcanic glass
   or tiny chip of shadow cast
ahead these centuries, somehow, through mine,
   into the unborn child's mind.

Escape

Window grid grey bird-net
stretched across my sleep. Dawn.
Wild turkeys feeding
underneath the orchard. One
is up a tree. Tap glass—
his comrades run.
And finally, and grudgingly,
a great umbrella beating open
in a close place,
he shakes the branchy heaven
from his wings,
and flies—

Thanksgiving

As likewise, uneclipsed,
the rising sun
escapes intact—
and later, too,
the lifting moon,
its breast curved up
like the white keel bone
left on the plate
when dinner's done,
the whiskey capped,
and everyone's gone home.

November

I keep watch as the green moon grows and gathers
in its shallow handblown basin. Another
month. This window is my compass rose;
I watch the earth swing north. The cirrus race
of atmosphere is mirrored here in gooseflesh skin;
the squint sun veers low and cooling, candles
distant snowclouds, slips the lake, the sky collapsing
after it, to embers, stars—
                                        Dark. The lapse
of light is longer now; December soon.
A struck match whips and frays, a tiny windsock
in these drafty rooms; flame grows, finds shelter
in the grey shells of soapstone stoves. Unsettled
over them, the house ruffs its reedy clapboards;
birds seek southering winds. Sequins
stitch the night from a dozen chimney fires and chain
the message south through town, and farther south, they plume
and fall, fail to root in the coughing channels
of the blood, the blood cooling towards
its long inconsequence—

Aubade

Cold snap. Five o'clock.
Outside, a heavy frost— dark
footprints in the brittle
grass; a cat's. Quick coffee,
jacket, watch-cap, keys.
Stars blaze across the black
gap between horizons;
pickup somehow strikes
its own dim spark— an arc—
starts. Inside, familiar
metal cab, an icebox
full of lightless air,
limns green with dash-light. Vinyl
seat cracks, cold and brittle;
horn ring gleams, and chrome
cuts hard across the wrist
where the sleeve falls off the glove,
as moon-track curves its cool tiara
somewhere underneath your sleep
this very moment, love—

Apples on Champlain

Oil-slick, slack shocks, ancient engine
smoking like a burning tire,
Augustus' old truck yaws and slews,
its leaf-springs limp these centuries
suspending apples, somehow pulls
the last hill past the bridge at Isle
La Motte. I hear the iron arches
groaning. Why not? Whole orchards
rattling, empty racks behind us,
emptied into grain sacks, piled
behind us— home ahead, we broach
the mile-long causeway cross from Grande Isle
back.
    A blue heron's motionless
in marsh grass to my right, and pole
and icepack at my left— one line,
two lanes, a roostertail of blue
exhaust, we part the cooling waters
of Champlain.
        The moon's a pool
of mercury. It's zero. Ice soon.
Steaming like a teacup, losing
heat, the lake is tossing clouds up
all around the truck; and tucked
so in its fragile ribcage creel,
the cold heart *thump* accordions
to keep alive, and fills, as apples
interrupt this landscape's black-
on-grey like heartbeats full of blood,
strung beads, a life of little suns
gone rolling down the press and sump
of memory and changing form
as *thump*, horizon groans and ladles
light, and the real sun comes up,
sudden, weightless, warm.

Gravity

Short chantey:
pull, then *pull*—
the chain-hoist rings
above a naked
cord-hung bulb
as burlap sacks
of apples filled
like lumpy ghosts
ascend the black
cobwebby air
inside the mill
until a split
seam pulls apart
and apples spill
and avalanche
the dark and flash
and send us skittering
like rats in rout
and the bare bulb
burns out

Unready

Season turns too fast for us:
we've cider in the cask;
Northern Spies wrapped in newsprint
may or may not last
all winter in the basement bins—
batten down. Bake pies.
Applejack is just as apt
to go to vinegar and back
as we are to be ready by
the time snow flies—

Apple Peeling; First Snow

Storm front shears
across the valley
black and slanting
as the hinged
wing blade hand-cranked
around this gear-work
apple peeler
swings around
its spindled pome;
and as this flayed skin
spirals off
a cooking apple's
flat green map
projected from
its northern pole,
now from the pole
swoop great wet flakes
the size of moth wings
spinning down
to white a globe
whose patterns in
the damp leaf litter
bleeding through
a moment later
leave its surface
just as brown.

Augustus Carries Fire

Autumn on to solstice,
all right— Old Man Winter's
damned druidical
theatrics: hot tongs, fierce
raptorial beak before
and spread peacock's plume
of sparks behind him damned
Augustus carries fire
from kitchen range to kindle
first flame for the winter
in his bedroom stove.
The only one I'll need,
he'll say. It won't go out.
I rage inside, I wring
my hands, I mince along
behind him like a child
on stepping stones. Damned
tinderbox here— buckets
of sand— pray for rain—
Charred bones we'll be.
We'll burn some day, old man's
fool inviolate customs
kill us, old fires banked
too deep inside the brain.

Dream

I juggle red apples
in this dream, at noon.
They rise like rushes
of the pulse
pushed up hard
from inner reaches
of the heart—
but soon, soon,
I must grow tired,
I must sit down,
and then I'll fling them one by one
past the far ridge
to blink the moon.

Orrery

To keep the deer away in deep
winter, I will decorate the bare
branches of the apple trees
with these small amulets of blood meal
wrapped and tied in cloth squares.
Queer charms, white ornaments,
they seem to stir the breeze a little,
they seem to stir the air.

Solstice

Christmas: quince, persimmon,
pomegranate, rose;
glass flowers twirling
in a glass case,
closed. A candle blown—

Now the world is locked and motionless.
Binoculars left on the sill are laced
with hoar frost— frozen compass rose.
The only color left across
this stark, inert field of view
is the red stem of the thermometer
itself. I watch it shrink back down
its bulb. This world will be too hard.
I press my wrist against
the bull's-eye windowpane a moment,
imagining my own blood
shrinking back along the glassworks
of the veinous system
to the heart.

In Vitro

Rosaceae: so read the case
we'd seen the apple blossom in,
and strawberry, a specimen,
and cinquefoil, too, displayed, in place,

each labelled in a long vitrine—
recall them: windrows, ranks and files
arranged in cool museum aisles,
a prism's red, and blue, and green—

each bloom a lens they might have plucked
before the lemur's eye could look,
or hold in focus, slowly twirl
as sand by starlight spun the world

the night the creaking case was closed,
and dust first settled on its dome,
and *apple* stirred, by thorn and pome,
the turning orrery of *rose*.

Aurora

Draco decorates
the orchard, low, and Vega
like a gas flame, steady
on the mountain's flank—
I say the names. It's reflex,
now; he echoes me. Tonight
we watch a thin aurora
percolating low
in this vicinity,
all nacreous and white,
no veils, no color in it—
again, again, it sleets
the purple dome down
and disappears— *soaks in,*
I'll say, say rennet staining
down some sleepy Asian
emperor's bejewelled
chemise. . . another pearl
strung. Bedtime tales.
His thousand nights. While I—

the urn of light
another story
each love's stain
and pattern left
of life
of semen leaping back
across the generations
cirrose light
struck off its starry plectrum
one way only
simultaneous
and everywhere
without the grace of sequence
in the spiral field
of memory
where old stars burn

47

beside the young
and features of the human face
return
return

The Full Snow Moon (Lullaby)

How can you sleep?
How can you keep
your eyelids closed
against the glare
of moonlit snow
across your starchy
pillow slip,
a snowfield steep
as one outside
where silhouetted
on the sky
are mountain spruces
gaunt as great
earthbound birds
asleep, at roost,
their ragged whiskbroom
wings fanned low
and full of ice,
and far below
a long fall
of shadows spilled
down from their feet
three hundred feet
to fields as flat
and white as salt. . . .
Inside, the hoar frost
feathers glass,
unfurls its unceils
sill and sash,
unforms, reforms
itself, is gone,
as breath against
the window steams
condensing on
the sleeper's lash
to weigh him down
again, to dream.

Champlain in Winter

Deep winter, crossing Lake Champlain. Here
the north wind is steadier than gravity;
it has a long sweep down from Canada
before it intersects the Grande Isle causeway.
Sawteeth: icicles all horizontal
off the guardrail cables— compass points,
each bearing south across the grey expanse,
where two linked forms unfrozen in the windsock
of the fog and telescoping whorl
of snow and scarcely visible at all
can just be brought to focus: *skidding deer
on crazed ice; light dog loping.*

News

Crumpled, wrapped in old newsprint,
the winter apple that I carry
up from its basement storage bin
reminds me of the cratered moon.
The moon itself resembles something
like a leaden IBM ball covered
with its alphabet of zeroes,
hanging still above the dead
glacial sheet of North America.
I see it coming down, I hear
the planet's stone plate struck and ringing
like a cymbals with some dread news—

News

No news. Wolf Moon.
Wife gone home.
Augustus tends his own omens
in his own room;
I tend the fires myself.
Fill the woodbox. Feed sheep.
Look for something she's
secreted on a kitchen shelf.
Eat alone. Sleep.

Storm

Late winter, waken alert in half-light, lie
still below the rustling slate. Slight
sound: an icecube ringing glass— no, steel
of course, a shovel blown to the concrete machine-
shed floor. The far rim of the universe is fifteen
yards away, where I can just make out, mid-arc,
the lash of branches where one sapling's wild elastic
radian defines this half of the grey half-dark.
I watch the little leashed bags of blood meal
whip and flail this strange easterly blaze
of rain-snow as though some old attraction laced
inside them stirs them now, like pith balls, bolas,
round and round and crazy for some mark—
say blood to the fresh heart's blood— or say the bare
bullet's tendency through unthreshed air
to seek heat, to seed the lively dark.

Died

Wind's died; no dream. Late supper; slept alone,
if slept; up early. Windows blank as wet slate
where snow's still falling on the world . . . I chip a saucer
(shaving in the kitchen sink— recidivist
since you've been gone) through the wrinkled skin of ice
across the frying pan and gravy bowl and plates.
Here water not quite lukewarm steams up off the soapstone
sink; my shaving mirror clouds in, mist
across the room behind, the eyes, the selvedge
of the skin obscure— a queer reverse
photography, the image unresolving . . . time lapse. Strop
Augustus' razor, touch its silver edge
a clear line on the cheek, groping for the soul
lost in the foggy glass— and cut myself,
of course. Observe how blood wells up in droplets,
runs, mixed grey with soap and tiny slivers
off the blade, and drop by drop falls, forms
circles in the stone sink—
                                        As clouds,
the storm sky—
                        As clotted nebulae, recalled
in silver iodide. . . . Lapsed time. I'd sooner
sleep without that dream, where I've seen rings form, widen,
lose all outline, and dissolve; seen
tracks circling, ravens, and the ringed sun's
own circlings somewhere high above this storm,
imagining the way Augustus died.

Dead Star

Black wreck this morning
steaming in a dirty
ring of ice
ammonia slush and char
and smoke and melted
concrete rebar Millard's
gambrel barn burned
middle of the night
last night no hope the hose truck
kept its steady
cataract of water
giving way to gunfire
six below
a dozen fat men
in sweaty undershirts
all running yelling
great balloons of breath
but one silent statue
still as he could be
except for eye-blink elbows
spastic back-and-forth
the pallid flashing
as he worked the bolt
such bellowing
count sheep pigs cows
see curved horns silhouetted
in the doorframes falling
stanchions sties
and bright-eyed Millard
watched his whole herd leap
out through the spindle
of his rifle sights
a dream a dream a dream
a dream roaring
in the ears
and the red sky
when Millard went to sleep
relieved of one fear
in his life at least

in all our lives
the sun caught in the screen
the skin the eye
the awful blooming in the east
and still no man has died

Winter's Tally

One murder
simple temper
shot him
one suicide
came up empty
mid-December
shot him
one manslaughter
crosshair gunsight
thought he was a bear
shot him
all by the moon, all by the moon
O hold the heavy cartridge gently
orange chrysalis sleeps lightly
in its brass cocoon

Sawmill

Snap tempered tooth chips
sawyer shouts *steel in sawlog*
lock engine off slack
line carriage back echo
like a gunshot ricochets
off galvanized tin roof the great
blade ringing like a gong
and every man down low:
look, along the log's sheer face,
the bright metal shows itself:
a tap, a nail, a bit of buried
wire, some wrong coordinate
or undetected intercept
exactly *there*— count the rings—
just forty years ago.

In Situ

No whisper of a sound this time,
no whine, no *snap*,
but echoes of a flat report
like distant ringing in the mind,
and this peculiar spore:
inlaid against the clear white sap-
wood, thick as a bolt,
bright as a blank undated dime,
a silver disk of metal shines.
Impossible!
It should have thrown the main belt,
unslung the boardsaw, left it smooth,
a toothless, stripped, tideless moon—
and this instead:
the sawyer pries it loose,
stands, extends
an open palm— a ragged scarab
out of time, a twist of lead
lies scarcely floating on the skin. . . .
What kind of archaeology
could hope to retrodict its arc
and dead trajectory again?—
say *when occurred,*
how accurate,
what impulse might have carried it
across these rings,
riflings
of green life spun between the bore
of blank heart-
wood at the core
and clear bluing of the future's barrel?
Threads cut. Pierced cocoon.
The tree gives no account.
The common artifacts
of fire, found as they are
everywhere, ubiquitous,
above the lively earth, below it, bear
no witness. False art,
they salt their site. Their

59

bearings come untrue, unfixed,
for always gunfire is intrusive
and its aims not always ours, its aims
far too facile, cool, untraced,
ill-starred—
for when is a bullet properly in place
if not in the rifled chamber,
if not in the chambered heart?

Speed of Light

The radium in luminescent numbers
painted on my watch face fades: no time,
and no things in the closed-in cosmos now
but these: the massive plow looming ahead,
the soft churn of chains in snow, eccentric
scythings of his hazard lights like amber
helicopter blades above, the close
cones of headlamps pressed against the blizzard's
high wall. I've followed him for miles now,
watched the spume combing off his cutwater,
the great V-plow, speeding, sparks spurting
underneath its tempered edge and drifting
up the windscreen now in strange and unfamiliar
constellations, changing—
                A universe
in one dimension only, love, this road:
the black trace reeling off his rear wheels here
like new creation dragging off its spool.
This is the limiting velocity:
I thread this white cloud chamber as I can,
I etch this line across what curvature
of space and time still separates us, now,
and night dilates, all night, all night the plow
grinds the stone road bed like my heart
grinding through this last bad month alone
without you, in the dark or in the light.

Dream

I dream I juggle yellow apples,
polished amber stones—
see, one by one they glow with light,
they rise like notes from oboes blown
around the birth
around the breath
that rising up the open night
unslips the sweet and heavy earth—
as we must do one day, in death,
together and alone.

Runes

Rain in winter.
All the apple branches
clack together in the moonlight now,
a perfect lacquered page,
black on white.
Wind tonight:
a pruning hook,
the crescent moon arcs
overhead. The orchard cracks—
and in the clear air of morning
twig and branch and limb and root
ruined: ice-slick, eyelash
littering the glass-strewn sclera
of the snowfield, black on white,
like runes.

Sugar Season

Sugarmaker's
rule of thumb:
it's time to tap
the third day
before the first
bluebirds
come back;
it's hard to catch.

Tap—
the bright drill twirls, and all the trees
like Chinese rings, connected now:
two hundred metal buckets hung,
a mile of plastic tubing stretched
and washed and coiled and cut and strung.
At last the arch is touched to fire.
First steam startles off the pan;
banjo strings *ping*, loose wires guyed
to the plumed barrel of the chimneystack,
a tall shako tilting in the fast
flume of February sky—

To March. The cold sun arcs
above us as the zinc
curve of a bucket handle
bites across the palm.
Snow falls. Streams
freeze. Even the tractor
seems weary now; we palm
the engine block for heat,
and drenched gloves send up clouds,
send rain—

     Now *rink rink rink*
rink buckets brim and fill
too fast for us, and spill.
The loose forest falls,
a cataract of sweet
ice-water through our fingers.

Sugar maples languish
in their dirty wrinkled
sheets, like patients, tubed
and draining; day in, day out,
flu— we too, sick,
sink through rotten snow
and bruise a knee and slash
a shin on a bucket's steel rim
and soak a leg and fill
a boot and every man
and woman here is grim—

To April. Snowdrops
biopsy
the frozen ground,
burst open— *pop*—
round rivets— spring:
the whole woodlot
changing subtly
draws sweet wind
around it, riffling
cotton shirtsleeves;
snow melts off
in rivulets
and *rink* and *rink*
and *rink* the drops
come slow, sour, green.
Augustus, solemn,
breaks a raw egg
in the pan,
pronouncing like
a holy man
last batch.
Pan cools.
Sap stops.

Waterlogger

Crazy; that's concensus, here. Comes here couple
of nights a month like a true lunatic, oxygen bubble
of a moon rising on his greying cue ball crew cut,
pale eyes, salvage logs, crazy Davy Crockett
smile, everything about him pale as the night expanding
now with a waxing moon like the croak in its air-sac, spawn-
track quivering the road, the blue marshlight flying out
from here, the farthest Magellanic Cloud no doubt
resounding to the tight translucent membrane in a bullfrog's throat—

Here comes the Navy now, across the moat.
Gears like dropped sledgeheads, suck of tires, two cast-eyed
headlamps fork the drowned yard's pocked and cratered mud-sty,
hundred puddles blinking back the moon. . . . This rain-sluiced,
hub-deep place might be the map in '38, when the last
true hurricane sheared through the Northeast, felled
a whole state forest overnight. On Roosevelt's
dollar they jacked the timber, trimmed it clear, skidded
it out to the nearest water hole. Clogged it; corduroyed
every local lake and fishpond, frog-fen, quarry pit;
quit. Steadier work was on its way; war. Spit.
The boles went down with the battleships at Pearl.

Tonight, this lumber yard's his eery boneyard. Look: burled
reptilian femurs dripping on the carriage, bleached white,
perfectly preserved these years, still the marrows sweet
wood, wet as celery, pluming water where the saw slips in—

Driving home, after midnight, I'll think of him.
Waterlogger: frogman home from the perfect blue Pacific,
fixing chains on a defunct forest in the murk and sieve
of the sky's dead bottom, hung on drowned fronds, eel-
grass feathering his groin, his chest, his cooling seal-
skin sack of bones bobbing sometimes in the slick caul
and surface-tension of reflected sky, schooling
clouds, live leaves, where water striders trace his spine—

He moves his webbed hands slowly, working blind.
As later, when a dream unfolds its old map, marsh and pond

and dragonfly and catkin world, where the mind's eye's opened
in the eye of the heron, crippled onto one leg, in the least
corner of the dream, one feels him stirring slightly, necklaced
in frog spawn, knees and elbows tucked against the sternum—

Or surfacing, where the dream's live drumhead plucks off, unmasks, numb
fingers clenching cowl, fins, naked cable, cray-
fish balanced on one shoulder, big face smiling like crazy
as the dream bursts, and the startled heron flies away.

Slater (Equinox)

Early morning
Saturday
my roofing ladder
at the peak
a light frost melting
into dew
across the slippery
low-pitched roof
and slating tools
in hand I lay
the blue-grey lichen-
crusted floor
of the Champlain Sea
so long extinct
above my sleeping
childrens' heads
and set the date
in green and red
for theirs (as may be)
standing on
some shell-pink shore
astride the ridge
of night and day
at dawn sometime
like this, to see—
the starry sky,
behind, before.

Shadow

Equinox
late sun
cold sky
scored plate
diamond point
pinned high
hyphen held
quick between
its own black shadow's
iron barrel
cast ahead
and vapor track
drawn out behind
white silk
scarf sleight
simple vector
day transmuting
out of night
or simple truth
rifling forward
through the eye
of its prediction
hard light
this Phantom carries
false dawn
hard change
its tiny prism
passing over
all our lives
and north across
the world and gone
the gauze fans out
and shreds in wind
and sun sets
behind the range
this fragile house
is pinned upon
such innocence.

Starling

Heard its drumming first downstairs:
no dream at all, a large bird loose
inside the room— an open flue.
It clatters, swoops the tilting house
and clears the lamps and loops somehow
to sanctuary, green— the turret
of the window bay a terror-
struck and echoing vitrine, whose
wilderness of hanging plants
swings sickeningly, wing-slammed, sley
on twisting thread, and plain-weave sash
struck hard, and birdlime everywhere;
it whites the map where he'll not land,
a veer of lost flight back and forth
from light to light— I duck, a scare-
crow, duck again and back away.
His beak, his breast, his wingbeats snare
across the glass like castanets
until I think the gimballed earth
itself begins to sway—

And I too down the chimney straight
into the ancient uncast net
of nightmare: tonight, again, *the punctured
greenhouse*: where, high and frail, a spun-
glass arboretum starts to vibrate,
touched, high up— a shard of chert
tic enters slowly like a small
star-drill, drifts down, transects the humid
chamber so, to kiss a far wall
tic, exploding outward in a plume
of glass— and hear, an insect-hum
inside the ear, the conch shell sounding
at the drum, where scimitars
of falling plate whir down and scythe
the dark and cooling space inside
the room, its delicate cloud forest
first laid bare, exposed for the first
time to the airless dark, to the steep

70

and penetrating light of stars,
where every green goes sepia,
goes brown, and consciousness whorls down
no lullaby, no dream, to sleep.

March Orrery

Listen:
pale beech leaves
branch-clung all winter long,
their tissues frail as paper lanterns,
lucent, ornamental, touch the pane.
Diminutive ribcages, curled and weightless,
slant along the axis of the rain,
touch *click*, click loose at random underneath
the eaves, and turn a brief descent, and skitter
one by one in wind, and gone, as quick
as shell-ice down an onion dome,
or unshared memory,
or old rice paper,
blown.

Easter

Great world's rocking like a cradle, listen—
seams bent open in the wind tonight,
the whole house trembling . . . outside, tines, antennae
singing on their mast, and trees in tune;
here too, wind drains up the chimney, rings
the room, disturbs the undrawn curtains, sucks
across the wine rack whistling like a syrinx
uncorked in the distance somewhere, stirs
your long skirt's hem, the candle flame, this Easter
dinner cooling on my lifting fork—
I fill your glass; the bottle drops a fourth.
Still green and cloudy, sweet, still working, apple
wine reminds me how the warm dark eases
life, and love; how small night-blooming orchids
touch the sticky gobbet of their pollen
to the feeding hawk moth's compound eye,
as how this night has touched its opalescent
moon against the many convex facets
of the window bay, each whorl and lens
reflecting back, and how the night sky
spilling through this house with dusty wings,
with wind, will find us in another Lenten
season, you and I, another fast
broken, another winter come to spring.

Driving Sleeping People

Home drive. High beams shearing brome grass,
blackcaps, brambles by the roadside;
red stems siphon frozen ground
grown soft, a bruise beneath the smooth suede
winter peach that rolls across
the dashboard. Thaw through frost. We pass
warm pockets now and then of sweet
spring air. Mount Equinox, Ascutney,
far ahead, still bear the weight
of ice, the Champlain Glacier's skirt
drawn back— imagine ancient beasts
suspended high, great woolly mammoths
half a mile above us cast
in ice, in time, the moon a beat
of fine rice paper wings—
                              White moths
are streaming to my windscreen, tracers
through the night that lies across
the sleeping globe tonight like thick
volcanic glass. One diamond scores
it. Somewhere sunrise, somewhere crows
lift off their power lines like quarter
notes suspended echoing
in mind again— such dark and lithic
deaths as lie ahead, smooth bulbs,
the denser black-in-black, dark knots
embedded in the grain of night
we pass through like a blade. I close
my eyes to this, to all impalpable
danger, now. They sleep, a nest
of starlings pooled into their own
black shadows in the back seat, sightless
son and daughter stir a moment,
mutter nothing, sleep again.
Against the door, an empty dress,
my wife, asleep, her face a surface
clear as water catching light
as cars flash by—
                              And I see what,

see changing patterns on the skin,
the wheel, this road, the pale surf
of mountains cresting in the starlit
distance, sea behind, its pull
and seiche inside us still, the trick
of centuries. We've measured Thuban,
Kochab, Vega, gone; Polaris
shining in its geometric
steeple somewhere east of north—
I feel its fixture in the dome,
the needles turning at the wrist,
the wheel for one extended moment
steady in my hand. . . . By earthlight
I feel this, the peace of this,
of driving sleeping people home.

Late Light

Late rain
drops smoked
glass smears
last light
gone God
damned plough
broke down
dark parts
stars now
clouds draw
long grey
gauntlet off
damp field
half clawed
corduroy—

Already called
to supper driver
visor up
back-crawls
chin to axle
blessed tractor
hitch cracked
crickets hiss
brass asp
caught between
asbestos fingers
spurts blue
acetylene
beside his cheek
where bluets droop
the whole scene
about to burst
shock pop
pock hiss
in the harsh lick
of oxygen—

A poppy-bloom
whose jillion sparks
across the ancient
genitive
illuminant
and soundless dark
have all come down
somehow to this
where liquid steel
slips like a slug
across a crack
below careening
galaxies
and slow segmented
Milky Way
where one lies flat
between gigantic
tractor wheels
in a wet black
half-ploughed field—

Where voice strains out
on yellow light
through the screen door
to call him back.

Plume

In the orchard,
puffs, plumes,
odd gusts—
when suddenly
the trees toss up
their blooms at once:
white petals
chimney up
and braid together
in the sky
like sweet smoke
from the same flame—
so beautiful!
And still, a shame.

Sweep

You'll hold the heavy
flap of canvas
hard against the hearth
once we begin. *O K*,
you say, if unconvinced.
Now rattling on the rooftop—
Ooo—hell-ooo—hell—ooo
he calls. I stoop
inside the hearth to hear
Augustus echo
down from heaven
through the speaking tube.
I grope and blink and peer.
The damper's open—
wait, I yell, and back
away, too late; too soon
he drops his rope
and burlap packed
with brick and chain,
a pendulum
swung down the ancient
well of hope
and anchor plumb
to parlor room;
it brooms the chimney *chink-*
chink, choked flue avalanching
loose at once, a hellish
rush, ash mushrooms
up like dried ink,
spiralling dead smoke,
old creosote
like light cicada
shell— whole rookeries
of old crows, desiccated
starlings skirling,
gusting here and there;
Augustus querulous
and warbling
above his empty rifled

79

flue *Clean sweep!*
                    Head crooked
beneath one wing I look
at you— where, love, you stare
into the mantel's mirror,
preen your quills—
they shawl your shoulders,
drift in mare's-
tails, back and fill,
they black your eyeblinks
in the dark
and decorate
your ruffled hair;
and you— *Say marry
me.* I do: *I will.*

Married

Swung door
one o'clock
black suit
shoes clack
on blue stones
where the great stained
window, blazing,
butterflies the floor.

Up Chimney

Legs extended to the room
like Yule logs; arms crossed; bare head pillowed
on the cool swept stone, the hearth
in summertime . . . I do this, sometimes,
staring up the flue, stargazing
fool, my heavy draftplate flipped back
like a visor on the view.
Eternity! Blue-black! Below—
an insect-crawl, a slow prickling
in the spot between the shoulder
blades—I almost feel Orion's
passage. China lies between us,
and eight thousand miles of ironware,
core and mantle. On the mantel-
piece, the moon is tipped up, balanced
like a broken plate. Thus, chin
on chest, I see the room's reflection
in the window bay six feet
beneath my shoes. I see you sideways
at your sewing table, needle
in your teeth; Aldebaran,
a beauty-mark, has risen to
your cheek. And rest my head again,
to scry the open chimneypot
above, where The Bird's white eye, Altair,
stabs back; it drifts across its tiny
square of sky and tracks The Arrow
north and west across the frame
into the black coal sacks at Cygnus,
blank spots in the Milky Way—
where I, too, blink back the spark,
grown fearful for an instant of
the pupils' unwilled spiralling,
their open merging with the dark—

In June

Now the earth is warmer than the air.
The eyes adjust, but slowly; for a while, still,
dark is all but absolute. Remember,
somewhere to our left, and close, a deer
woke up. He came out of his dream disturbed
and curious; we heard him stand, stamp,
snorting, close, hooves jarring through our backs
and ribcages like heartbeat in the ground,
and let our breath out long and slowly as we
could, and held—
     I felt your throat catch air—
as though the heart could hold its teacups-full
quite motionless above this pearly planet
here, oh, how we rattle, and I nearly
laughed out into that queer dark that leaves
the unconcerned household of the flesh
so clamorous—
     We lay a long while yet.
The night was sweet with timothy we'd crushed,
and uncut all around us so, it seemed
to rise like grey earth light. In time, it might
have cast our single shadow out among
the summer stars. This was in June. The stars
adjust. The moon had not then risen, but
its turbid light welled up and billowed like
a cool current furled in warmer water,
which appeared to stir some clouds a little,
water lilies on the near horizon—

Then the dream: that you had moved away,
had balanced there and let your legs into
that light, cool scarves of it across your open
lap and belly and throat and thrown-back cheek—
and the planet strung, then, crescent in the curve
between your spine's arch and the straight line, nightfall,
black hair back to earth.
     The deer has gone
up in some new and unlit constellation
by this time, and all his timothy

turned milk, or corn, or antler-silk torn loose
on a tall tamarack; and we have changed, as well,
and yet— the memory is so strong now
it startles me a moment, lying here,
my arms around you, not to feel the slight
wax-quilled insignature, the water-mark,
the grass impression on your shoulder blades
and strangely perfect back.

Solstice

      Dusk.
    Apple trees arachnid
in the valley's crawling shadow;
   high up, red-shouldered hawks
   slide wheeling, wheeling slowly
through the last Jacob's ladder,
   reeling rock and shadow
   up the windlass into
      night.

Dream

In this dream, my trousers rolled,
I juggle purple apples, low,
at sunset, some eons ago.
In this dream I'm old; I yawn;
I wade a salt marsh on this farm
while all around me eelgrass waves.
I feel the rustling of the moon
in restless sand beneath my feet.
It undermines me, feel its tide—
the last draining of the Champlain Sea.
A few stars bleed through the purple sky.
Now night comes on like cautery—
I turn around, and I can't see—
A cold sun bobs in brackish water,
knotted vein behind my knee.

Katahdin

Telephone: Augustus gone.
Oh, every year he's made this trip,
now damn fool's missing on the mountain—
eighty-six this spring, the mountain
closed for fog, unsafe, rangers'
warnings up, and still he'd
have to go again, his *once more*
up Katahdin. Idiot
set off alone, he always did,
oh, I can hear him, *know Katahdin*
better than the orchard, dentures
dropping on his words. The ranger
asked his favorite places— *Chimneys*,
Chock-stone— he's inclined to bushwhack
though, and strong, still. Chances
good they say. They'll call back soon.
We've sun, still, light late—
cool nights— twenty dozen deadfalls
in the fog— who knows. Wait.

Call

Fog's lifted. Dogs found where he left the trail.
Pack lunch; I'll leave by noon. Search parties out
since six o'clock, all local, volunteers
from the mills of Millinocket, Appalachian
Trail men, rangers. I think a few of Augustus'
friends from town may drive north, too. A special
helicopter search has been arranged,
to start at dawn, unless we find him first.
Ranger said a hurt man holes up, hides,
finds a den. *Look up,* he said— odd patterns
in the birds' flight, cries— *sometimes they mark
a man, sometimes you'll spot your man that way.*
I think of the square grid of the survey map,
the helicopter's swoop, the birds riding
thermals through the cooling air, conducting
their own search. I think of the miles of wilderness
park pooled around Katahdin in the dark.

Heart

To waste a life like this I can't forgive
Augustus this good Christ a friend and neighbor
nightmare nothing but the kindness in
his heart he'd volunteered he'd driven through
the night for this it happened halfway up
the mountain wasn't steep but open slope
and single file and slow with Millard leading
Irwin close behind I followed close oh
the man crumpled as I watched no warning fell
it was as though his legs dissolved in air
it wasn't like a falling man I felt
the hair rise underneath my collar caught
my wits then kneeling down beside him started
on the breathing. No time elapsed at all
so hoping for the best I told his two scared
sons to go for help fast they half fell
down Katahdin sliding scree combing
underneath their boots and all this time
I counted breaths and beat his chest down sixty
times a minute but it went on far
too long an hour I think I breathed him air
imagining his brain alive asleep
ribs broke and blood flecks in the mouth a ranger
came and tried to help got sick quit
the next time I looked up was into the beating
helicopter. Doctor took him turned
told me massive cardiac arrest
the heart muscle must have practically
exploded dead before he hit the ground
dead all that time. I drove straight back. What time
is it? I've washed I've got the smell of him
it's on my hands I'm speeding still I know
I'll slow down soon he should have known he knew
his own heart my God the man was only
fifty years what grief one son drove down
with me we drove all night no sleep no talk
Augustus never will be found God damn him
please forgive this weeping this is anger.

89

Dream

In my last dream
I juggle blue apples
on a mountain slope.
The snow is lightly falling,
and my epaulets are snow.
I seem to see
the blue globe settle
like a bubble
on my shoulder,
so.

The Starry Night

Another year, just so. Review:
Orion gone
with the northern lights, as all light leaching
quickly now;
I check my watch— it's nearly ten—
and turn to the changing
sky again. The once and future
polestars puncture
through. Thuban, Kochab, Vega,
compassing
the icecap, each chert stylus *tic-*
tic-tic
in zeroes figured long ago,
to thread the world's
magnetic iris, anchoring
its stars awhile. . . .
I think of Vega's blue beacon
mirrored here,
enamelled in the Champlain Glacier's
melting sheet,
or fixed into a vaulted arch
at Altamira,
Font-de-Gaume, when ochers sifted
through Lascaux. . . .
A sky-blink, *tic, tic—*
                    Time, now, ten
sharp, eyes a sluiceway
whistling with magnesium,
reports, salutes,
a cloud of burning metal salts—
my children follow
long stems up and watch them burst
and star and fall,
a sleet of fire. My son's embarrassed
later on;
an ember lights his cheek, his arm;
it's nothing, skin
a paper lantern-cloth, and earth
is unfamiliar

to him still, and so he cries.
Just now I think
we've watched five billion years break by,
seen novas flaring,
all the heavy atoms thickened
deep inside
the ancient stars— seen all the stuff
of man and earth
come sifting down the sky to stove-
black here, and hearth-
stone here. The urn of light. An iron
sun's repose.
So vapor trails collapse to roses,
rise, and burn,
and set again. Who counts the blank
spots in the sky?
But these are who we are, who lie
across coarse blankets
here, as I did by my father
on the Fourth,
another life of warm Julys.
The stars blink out.

Show's over; time to go. The sleight
of fire that jewels
the dark in memory is done;
daughter, son
lie fast asleep. I lift my wrist
where the sweep hand glows
and stand, yawning, yearning too—
for life maybe,
a figured sky, the high falsework
of the light
that arches under heaven's fall—
and feel the drift
of ash, the sieve, that limes the sleeper's
upturned eye,
that sleeves us all in time, in time.

PHYSICS

in Riddles,

for Mary

How many suns
will cross its coign
before the last
freeze? What
pennywhistle
spun its point
on the glass
breeze? Whose
airs are loosened
in the pane
like miniature
degrees, where
breath condenses
into rain
among the apple
trees? Here
tesserae
have turned to earth,
here blossoms may
attend to birth
as sun becoming
leaves; here
branches seem
to lead the glass,
whose scenes compose
as seasons pass,
the lifetime, piece
by piece. . . . A sphere

Begins and ends:
suppose, as glaciers
drop their catch,
as memory's
a ragged seine,
as grain by grain
a dead morraine
the sky is softly
sifting ash,
as constellations
each rescind
to embers, umbral
lees— alas,
the crown lens
will surely tear
to end the long,
sweet refrain
of sun to moon
to sun again,
of E from M
C²—
and then what breath
once shaped the pane
may lose itself
(we pray) in airs
our children, too,
had breathed in time,
and theirs, and theirs.

If oracles
recall in riddles
orreries
in orreries,
the quantum of
the apple's arc
the piper's tune,
the dancer's turning
crown of sonnets
in the dark
by starlight ground
between the querns
spun withershins
of dawn and dusk
to wreathe a green
and weathered earth—
it's moonshine, love,
and loneliness.
Do looney jigs
unwind the suns?
Might jugglers drop them
every one?
Are seeds resewn,
or tales respun?
When pipers stop
to play the bones
the very stones
are left undone.

To please the Sphinx
all life unreels
through black magnetic
stone-strewn fields
where pitchblende blinks
its slow decay
tic-tic-tic
de-lightedly
by alpha, beta,
gamma, delta—
time dilates
and starlight bends
in gravity
like roundelays.
All light, partic-
ulate, licks out
one way, in waves;
electric clouds
expand in spheres
whose uncracked shells
concentrically
unrecalled
across the parsecs
and the years
ring out, shift red
(like Hell), disperse
the edges of
the universe—

Eclectic quarks
a dish collects
to parse into
initial text—
miraculous,
exotic sky!—
a Book of Kells
whose quirkish tale
in optical
if stale effects
is mirrored in
the lemur's eye,
as through the hatchling's
candled egg
comes first light to
the cockerel—
As Sol dissolves
against the clock,
and seismographic
needles track,
and continents
incline to raft,
uranium
sines off to lead
or raindrops pock
a full carafe
to lilypads
inside the head—

Assymmetries:
no wave contracts—
a tracer's seam-
less, sequinned *O,*
or stoned window's
cataract—
What echoes in
the ears of bats,
frail globes of light
colliding back?
Kaleidoscopes
reshuffle shards,
toc, starred;
tic, intact—
let's retrodict
the apple's fall,
the reel's hiss,
the needle's spin;
the pin-gears on
the color wheel
feel artificial
after all;
let's kiss the dice
behind the eyes
and finish this
where it begins—
the empyrean's
synchesis:

Now ask why seasons
follow sequence,
green to red
or red to blue,
while life re-seeds
back through the snow
like pattern bleeding
into hue;
how particles
of colored sand
sift back a shaman's
circling fist,
as first riddled
suns-at-seed
spun out this creaking
artifice—
Would sonnets turned
at light speed
cooper square
in their vitrines?
Or meter's super-
sonics trace
a breath against
a mirrorscape
where starlight's slow
as clotted cream,
and every scheme
anticipates?

A stich in time:
where earth has cooled,
antique tectonic
shelves awash
in tepid seas
whose milky chyme
has knit such spiral
molecules
as struck off copies
of themselves
(*O miracle!*)—
and what's occurred
but stray elec-
trical discharge
between some cloud
and neaping tide
still arcs inside
the notochord. . . .
Who knows when first
aortic arches
registered
an ocean's surge,
or slipped awake
or stirred asleep;
how many tides
had ebbed until
the tiny seahorse
heart could leap?

And here Odysseus'
dazzled seas,
his charts, his quilled
geodesy:
where suns have fallen
grain by grain—
according to
what codicil?—
like yellow pollens,
sill and pane;
where Coriolis
forces cause
the cosmic dust
to curl down drains
whose gravities
call back for us
across the years,
like sea to rain. . . .
Where, streaming tails
of phosphorus
dead-center through
the Ferris whorls
and net-work of
the window's seine,
white moons like minnows
slip its sash
into the seiche
inside the brain—

A seer's odd
sensation: say
why dawn should follow
each saccade,
Charybdis' widened
irides
contract again
from west to east,
a narrow-waisted
fall of sand
or hollow winestem
once released
between two fingers
of what hand,
its syrinx sounding
centuries. . . .
And here the Masters
of Lascaux
pinched out an earth
and shaped a sky
inside a mountain
years ago—
time out of mind,
we say— just so,
rebounding echoes
fade to rhyme
across an inch,
an age, and die—

Of course he's blind,
whose achromatic
lenses frame
his myths around
a perfect scale
of azimuths
and measured time—
touch the braille:
a moth wing brushed
to prism's flame,
a telescope's
collapsing torch
astronomers
routinely scry,
or pipers, jack-tars,
all the same:
to ask true numbers
of the night,
to know the cauter
of the day—
one star resolving,
silver, high,
another disk,
another, then
a cataract
of viscous light,
a stack of coins
against the eye—

And what attractive
force is this?
Coincidence,
et cetera—
full moons inset
and stacked like plates;
the planets nested
flat as spoons—
a satyr-play.
Ah, love, instead,
let's study love;
it's getting late.
As geomantic
curvatures
may cup the clanking
cosmos in,
a sparking censer's
pendulous
and fragrant arc—
as space depends
on fob-chains which,
if charmed and real
are wholly im-
material—
then we, I think,
are amateurs,
and life a mys-
tery to feel:

If jugglers are
geometers
and pennywhistles
cost a dime;
if planets on
their abacus
click back to us,
tic back, because
the open skies
in memory
are perpendic-
ular to time—
one purple night's
a gemmary
of all nights figured
by design
across our sleep
in ores as rare
as any dust-motes
in the mine
of empty space—
an orrery
whose imperfection
in the mind
of which jongleur
you've married (who?)
reflects in these
beriddled lines:

As ephemer-
ides of blue
and red and green
are held apart
caparisoning
simple truth
seen bending through
the prism's bars—
as light unrav-
elling reveals
such orreries,
ascending, starred,
as unify
into a field
where dream dilates
and glass extrudes
and sonnets draw
like taffy through
a compass-needle's
eye— this chart
is scanned in light
of you, of you,
the physics he's
accustomed to,
the gravity
against his heart,
whose art again
begins for you.

RICHARD KENNEY was born in Glens Falls, N.Y., in 1948 and graduated from Dartmouth College in 1970. His poetry has been widely published and has attracted honors, among them the narrative poetry prizes from the Poetry Society of America and from the *New England Review and Bread Loaf Quarterly*, and three of the annual prizes awarded by *Poetry* magazine. In 1983 his first book, *The Evolution of the Flightless Bird*, won the 79th Yale Series of Younger Poets competition, judged by James Merrill. A Guggenheim Fellow for 1984–5, Mr. Kenney currently lives in Seattle with his wife, Mary Hedberg. His family home is in Middletown Springs, Vermont.